NOW
THAT'S
FUNNY

JOKES FOR KIDS

Other books by Sandy Silverthorne

Crack Yourself Up Jokes for Kids
More Crack Yourself Up Jokes for Kids
Made You Laugh!

NOW THAT'S FUNNY

451 Side-Splitting
JOKES FOR KIDS

SANDY SILVERTHORNE

SPIRE

Published by Revell
a division of Baker Publishing Group
PO Box 6287, Grand Rapids, MI 49516-6287
www.revellbooks.com

Printed in the United States of America

Library of Congress Cataloging-in-Publication Data
Names: Silverthorne, Sandy, 1951– author.
Title: Now that's funny : 451 side-splitting jokes for kids / Sandy Silverthorne.
Description: Grand Rapids, Michigan : Revell, a division of Baker Publishing
    Group, [2021]
Identifiers: LCCN 2020056326 | ISBN 9780800737672 (paperback) | ISBN
    9781493430567 (ebook)
Subjects: LCSH: Wit and humor, Juvenile.
Classification: LCC PN6166 .S575 2021 | DDC 818/.602—dc23
LC record available at https://lccn.loc.gov/2020056326

The author is represented by WordServe Literary Group www.wordserveliterary.com.

21 22 23 24 25 26 27   7 6 5 4 3 2 1

To Vicki—my wife, best friend, and true love.
You are truly a gift from God. Without you
I wouldn't be doing any of this. They say kids laugh
over 400 times a day. I'd say we're pretty close.

To Christy—you are the best. It's been so fun to
watch you grow up loving God and other people.
And thanks for sending so many jokes my way;
I really appreciate it!

To the kids I get to speak to every year—
you guys always make me laugh. Keep it up!

Introduction

Why did the kid drop veggies all over his map of the world? He wanted peas on earth. Now that's funny! What do cows read at breakfast? The mooos-paper. Now that's funny too! What do you call a bunch of little dogs with cameras? Pup-arazzi! Now that is REALLY funny!

Congratulations! You have in your hands the silliest, funniest, craziest, laugh-filled book on the planet! At least I think so. It's full of jokes, riddles, funny stories, one-liners, and knock-knocks that will definitely have you FOFL (falling on the floor laughing). It's also packed with crazy, silly illustrations and cartoons throughout.

What kind of fish fixes your grand piano? A piano tuna.

Now that's funny!

Also, you'll get a chance to test your tongue-twisting talent with tons of the toughest tongue twisters around. Like this:

Six slimy snails slid slowly seaward.

If you've ever dreamed of being a comedian, this is a great way to start. Try these hilarious jokes and one-liners out on your friends, family, and even your teachers.

Knock, knock. Who's there? *Venice.* Venice who? *Venice this door going to open?*

Wow, look at this: A truck loaded with vapor rub overturned on the freeway yesterday. Oddly enough, there was no congestion for eight hours.

Now that's funny!

So get ready to giggle, snicker, chuckle, guffaw, snort, crack up, and hoot. And definitely get ready to say,

NOW THAT'S FUNNY!

Q: What do you call a hen who can count her own eggs?

A: A mathemachicken.

Q: What do you call George Washington's false teeth?

A: Presidentures.

Dan: Where did Noah keep the old bees?
Jan: In the ark-hives.

Misty: What kind of bull is the cutest?
Christy: A dor-a-bull.

Logan: What do you get when you cross a police
dog with a skunk?

Rogan: Law and odor.

Q: Why did the silly guy put a fir tree in his living room?

A: He wanted to spruce up the place.

What do you
think of it?

Q: How do you make a strawberry shake?

A: Take it to a scary movie.

Q: What do you call a grumpy cow?

A: Mooo-dy.

Q: What's the coldest tropical island?

A: Brrr-muda.

Tongue Twisters

Randy's lawn rake rarely rakes really right.

I saw Susie sitting in a shoeshine shop.

A skunk sat on a stump and thunk the stump stunk,
   but the stump thunk the skunk stunk.

Background, background, black, black, brown, brown.

Near an ear, a nearer ear, a nearly eerie ear.

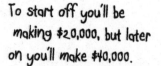

Jack: How does the man in the moon hold up his pants?

Zach: With an asteroid belt.

Mason: What do you call a GPS on a battleship?

Jason: A Navy-gator.

Donny: What do you call a pirate who skips classes?

Lonny: Captain Hooky.

Optometrist: Your results aren't very good.

Patient: Can I see them?

Optometrist: Probably not.

The butcher couldn't reach the meat on the top shelf. Apparently, the steaks were too high.

Ted: What kind of cats like to go bowling?
Ed: Alley cats.

Terry: What is Kate's clone's name?
Jerry: Dupli-Kate.

Rowan: What did the speaker at the gardening convention say to the audience?
Ava: "Please be seeded."

Knock, knock.
Who's there?

Cousin.
Cousin who?

Cousin stead of opening the door, you're making me stand here.

Q: What should you take on a journey through the desert?

A: A thirst-aid kit.

Sal: What do you call it when you eat a
banana sundae really fast?

Hal: Lickety-split.

Q: Where can you find a snowman's website?

A: On the winternet.

Q: What sports are trains good at?

A: Track events.

Asher: What would you do if a rhino came at
you at 60 miles an hour?

Connor: I'd do 70 miles an hour!

Alsea: Why are you giving your bees away?
Max: They're free-bees!

Knock, knock.
Who's there?

Venice.
Venice who?

Venice this door going to open?

Isabel: How do you get rid of a boomerang?

Rose: You throw it down a one-way street.

Knock, knock.
Who's there?

Isaiah.
Isaiah who?

Isaiah nothing until you open this door.

Knock, knock.
Who's there?

General Lee.
General Lee who?

General Lee, I don't tell knock-knock jokes.

Joe: Don't ever share secrets in a garden.

Flo: Why not?

Joe: Because the potatoes have eyes, the corn has ears, and the beanstalk.

Knock, knock.
Who's there?

Formosa.
Formosa who?

Formosa the summer, I was away on vacation.

Knock, knock.
Who's there?

Butcher.
Butcher who?

Butcher little arms around me and give me a hug.

Knock, knock.
Who's there?

Heidi.
Heidi who?

Heidi food; a bear's coming!

Chloe: What's big and gray and goes up and down?
Kylie: An elephant on a pogo stick.

Q: What kind of trucks do sheep drive?
A: Ewe-Hauls.

Q: What time is it when you go to the dentist?
A: Tooth-hurty.

Knock, knock.
Who's there?

Danielle.
Danielle who?

Danielle at me; it's not my fault!

Knock, knock.
Who's there?

Jewell.
Jewell who?

Jewell be sorry if you don't open the door!

Q: What do you call a police officer's uniform?

A: A lawsuit.

Q: How do you know when the moon is going broke?

A: When it's down to its last quarter.

Q: What kind of stories do pigs tell their kids at bedtime?

A: Pig-tales.

Q: Why was the mother firefly unhappy?

A: 'Cause her kids weren't very bright.

A guy just threw milk at me. How dairy!

Bill: Why did the wagon wheels go to jail?
Will: 'Cause they held up a stagecoach.

Matt: Why did the gingerbread boy stay home
from school?
Pat: 'Cause he felt crummy.

One night a little boy just wouldn't go to bed. Over and over, he asked his mom for one more drink of water. Finally, his mom said, "I don't want to hear you call 'Mom' one more time!" A little while later, a small voice called out from the boy's room, "Mrs. Taylor, could I have a drink of water?"

Lyle: What's white and can't climb trees?
Kyle: A refrigerator.

I got mugged by six dwarves this morning. Not Happy.

Sal: Did you see today's paper?
Hal: No, what's in it?
Sal: My lunch!

Remy: What do you call a hot dog bun that everyone looks up to?
Isabel: A roll model.

Q: Where did Captain Hook buy his hook?
A: At the secondhand store!

I can't use "beef stew" as a password on my computer. It's not stroganoff.

An odd chick is called egg-centric.

    Ed: I don't trust those trees over there.
Ned: Why not?
    Ed: They look a little shady.

Charlotte: What do you call a chick going on an
ocean voyage?

Rose: An egg-splorer.

City Guy: What do you call a cow that doesn't give milk?

Farmer: An udder failure.

Bob: Why did people think the big cat was lazy?

Rob: He was always lion around.

Nate: Are balloon animals smart?

Jonah: No, they're airheads!

Q: Where do you take a sick horse?

A: To the horse-pital.

Brian: Are those curtains real?
Ryan: No, they're drawn.

Jon: What are twins' favorite fruit?
Ron: Pears!

Mike: What kind of bread has the worst attitude?
Ike: Sourdough.

Tongue Twisters

Crisp crusts crackle and crunch.

Six slimy snails slid slowly seaward.

Cooks cook cupcakes quickly.

On a lazy laser raiser lies a laser ray eraser.

Red lorry, yellow lorry.

Q: What does Mickey Mouse listen to on his way to work?

A: Car-tunes.

Son: Dad, I'm just like Washington, Jefferson, and Lincoln!

Dad: Why's that?

Son: I went down in history.

Hannah: What kind of car does a cat drive?
Deagan: A Fur-rari.

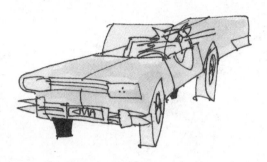

I shook my family tree and a bunch of nuts fell out.

Q: What do you call pasta that has no friends?
A: Ravi-lonely.

Q: Why can't Christmas trees sew?

A: They keep dropping their needles!

Q: How do frogs make breakfast?

A: They use a toad-ster!

Q: What do you call a lamb who dances?

A: A Baaa-lerina.

Is an argument between two vegetarians still called a "beef"?

Q: How much does Santa pay to park his sleigh?

A: Nothing. It's on the house!

My class took a field trip to the soft drink factory. We had a pop quiz afterward.

I have a fear of giants. The doctor says I have fee-fi-phobia.

Max: What's the world's largest onion called?
Jax: A ton-ion.

I love my fingers; I can always count on them.

We should call veterinarians "dogtors."

Someone stole my lamp. Now I'm de-lighted.

Asher: What do you call it when it rains ducks and chickens?

Harper: Fowl weather.

Rowan: How do vegetables say goodbye?
   Ava: "Peas out."

Q: What did Mars say to Saturn?
A: "Give me a ring sometime."

Jason: What do you call a sloppy hippo?
Mason: A hippopota-mess.

Mack: Why did the ancient Egyptians like to
     shave their heads?
Mike: To be more Pharaoh-dynamic.

Q: What do you call five giraffes?

A: A high-five.

Tad: Where do pirates keep their cookies?

Rad: In a cookie *JAAARRRR*!

Mike: Do you want to talk about infinity?
Deagan: No, I'll never hear the end of it.

Caden: What do you call a rabbit comedian?
Alsea: A funny bunny.

A funny thing HOPPENED to me on the way over here . . .

Office Worker: I hear music coming out of my printer.

Intern: Oh, the paper's jammin' again.

Q: How does a snowman get to work?

A: By icicle.

If the shoe fits . . . buy another one just like it.

Q: What do you call a bunch of little dogs with cameras?

A: Pup-arazzi.

Q: Where do sheep buy their cars?

A: At ewes' car lots.

Research says that 70 percent of the population is really dumb. I must be in the other 40 percent.

A man rushes into a doctor's office.

Man: Doctor, do you have anything for hiccups?

Doctor: I sure do.

He grabs a glass of ice-cold water and throws it in the man's face.

Doctor: How's that? Did it do the trick?

Man: I don't know. It's for my wife out in the car. She's the one with the hiccups.

Bill: What does a baby computer call its father?

Phil: "Data!"

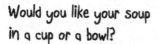

Q: What do you call one of Santa's helpers who is rich?

A: Welfy.

Hannah: What do cows read at breakfast?

Bo: The mooospaper.

Bill: Should you have your entire family for Thanksgiving dinner?

Jill: No, we'll just stick with turkey.

Caden: Did you hear about the actor who fell through the floorboards?

Braedon: No, what happened?

Caden: Nothing. He was just going through a stage.

Q: What do you call a sleepy fruit?

A: A nap-ricot.

Max: What do you call an elephant in a VW Bug?
Alsea: Stuck.

Farm Kid: What does it mean when you find a
        horseshoe?
City Kid: Some poor horse is walking around in
        his socks!

Q: What do you call a snowman's temper tantrum?

A: A meltdown.

Q: What's a snowman's favorite game?

A: Ice Spy.

Ice spy . . .

Connor: If athletes get athlete's foot, what do astronauts get?

Kylie: Missile toe.

Q: What does a farmer wear in the fall?

A: A har-vest!

Ed: What do you get when you drop a pumpkin from the sixth floor?

Ned: A squash.

Pat: Why are skeletons so calm?

Matt: Because nothing gets under their skin.

Q: Who leads all the apples to the bakery?

A: The Pie Piper.

Kylie: What do you call it when a tree goes on vacation?

Harper: Paid leaf.

Q: What's a chick's favorite drink?

A: Peepsi-Cola.

Q: What did Obi-Wan Kenobi say in the restaurant?

A: "Use the fork, Luke."

Q: Why did the Easter egg hide?

A: He was a little chicken.

Logan: Why is your dog staring at me?

Rogan: Maybe 'cause you're eating out of his bowl.

Q: **What do librarians take with them when they go fishing?**

A: Bookworms.

Saw an ad for an old radio for just a dollar—said the volume was stuck on high. I said to myself, *I can't turn that down.*

Q: What happened to the chick that acted up in school?

A: She was egg-spelled.

Chloe: Why is your fish wearing a soccer uniform?

Connor: He's my goal-fish.

Pat: What do you call an egg that's always playing tricks on people?

Matt: A practical yolker.

Q: What do you call a doe caught in a storm?

A: A rain-deer.

Lyle: Why is it hard to have a conversation with a goat?

Kyle: 'Cause they're always butting in.

Oh, that reminds me of a story...

Jack: Why did the rooster cross the road?

Zach: He needed to cock-a-doodle-do something.

Sal: Why did no one play games with the big cat on the ark?

Hal: 'Cause they knew he was a cheetah.

CHEETAH!!

Q: Why did the duck fall down on the sidewalk?

A: It tripped over a quack.

Q: What do you take before every meal?

A: A seat.

Q: How does the sky pay its bill?

A: With a rain check.

Randy: Never tell a burrito a secret.
Andy: Why not?
Randy: They might just spill the beans.

I ran into twin octopuses—they were i-tentacle!

**Q: What falls down in the winter but never gets
hurt?**

A: Snow.

I tried working for a pool maintenance company, but
the job was too draining.

Q: What did one volcano say to the other volcano?

A: "I lava you!"

Joe: What time is it when the clock strikes thirteen?

Bo: Time to get a new clock.

Bill: What do you get when you cross a pie with a snake?

Will: A pie-thon.

Ryan: What kind of dog is the best artist?

Brian: A labra-doodler.

Q: What kind of motorcycle does Santa ride?

A: A Holly-Davidson.

Ron: Who's a penguin's favorite aunt?
Jon: Aunt Arctica!

I'm so good at sleeping, I can do it with my eyes closed.

Caden: Who loves hamburgers, fries, and ants?
Alsea: Ronald McAardvark!

Doctor: Have you been sleeping with an open
window like I suggested?

Patient: Yes.

Doctor: So, is the congestion gone?

Patient: No. So far, the only things that are gone
are my laptop and my flat-screen TV.

Brian: When I drink coffee, I can't sleep.

Ryan: Wow, I have just the opposite problem.

Brian: Really?

Ryan: Yeah. When I sleep, I can't drink coffee.

Q: How do mountains stay warm in the winter?

A: They wear their snowcaps.

Q: What is a little dog's favorite dessert?

A: Pup-cakes!

I was going to tell you the fruit-drink joke, but I forgot the punch line.

I didn't like my beard at first. Then it grew on me.

Len: I just got a job at a bakery.
Ben: Why's that?
Len: I kneaded the dough.

I wish more people were fluent in silence.

Tongue Twisters

If Stu chews shoes, whose shoes should Stu choose?

Sheena leads, Sheila needs.

Tie twine to three tree twigs.

I wish to wash my Irish wristwatch.

Thin grippy, thick slippery.

What are you doing with that badge?
You're a pumpkin!

I'm a security gourd.

Q: What do you get when you cross a great white shark with a computer?

A: A mega-bite.

Be kind to your dentist—after all, he has fillings too.

Q: Why are frogs always so happy?

A: They eat whatever bugs them.

I dig, you dig, he digs, she digs, they dig. Not a great poem, but it's really deep.

Did you hear about the astronaut who hated tight places? He just needed a little space.

I'm going out for some fresh air.

Q: What does a nosy pepper do?

A: Gets jalapeño business.

**Q: What is an astronaut's favorite part of a
   computer?**

A: The space bar.

That scary French bakery gives me the crepes.

Q: Why did the Oreo go to the dentist?

A: He lost his filling.

I got my wife a refrigerator for her birthday. I can't wait
to see her face light up when she opens it.

The rotation of the earth really makes my day.

Asher: Why did the nurse bring a red pen to work?

Harper: In case she needed to draw blood.

Q: What do you call a train carrying bubble gum?

A: A chew-chew train.

Q: Why should you never tell a secret to a pig?
A: It's bound to squeal.

Q: What's in the middle of a gummy bear?
A: A jelly button.

Q: What do you call a guy who used to dig ditches?
A: Doug.

Escalators don't break down—they just turn into stairs.

Rob: How did Benjamin Franklin feel when he discovered electricity?

Bob: He was shocked!

Bob: Why are you hitting that cake with a hammer?

Rob: It's a pound cake.

Bill: Why did the whale cross the ocean?
Will: To get to the other tide.

Q: What does a bee use to cut wood?
A: A buzz saw.

Q: Who's the smartest bird in the world?
A: Owlbert Einstein.

Q: What state has the most cats and dogs?
A: Pets-ylvania.

Teacher: If chickens get up when the rooster crows, when do ducks get up?

Devon: At the quack of dawn.

Knock, knock.
Who's there?

Amos.
Amos who?

A mosquito just bit me.

Q: What kind of car does an egg own?

A: A Yolkswagen!

Dan: What happened when the strawberry crossed the road?

Jan: There was a traffic jam.

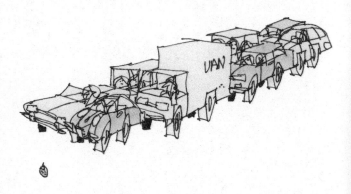

Q: What do you call a cow that's run out of milk?

A: A Milk Dud.

I just took a picture of a wheat field. It came out a little grainy.

Caden: Does your dog have a license?
Max: No, I never let him drive.

Farmer's Son: One cow, two cows, three cows, four cows . . .
Farmer: What are you doing?
Farmer's Son: Cownting.

Q: What kind of lions are the best swimmers?

A: Sea lions.

I'm starting a chicken-feed business. I'm just waiting for some seed money.

A truck loaded with vapor rub overturned on the freeway yesterday. Oddly enough, there was no congestion for eight hours.

I do all my addition in my head. It's the thought that counts.

Q: What time is it when ten lions are chasing you?

A: Ten after one.

Q: What kind of fish only appears at night?

A: A starfish.

**Q: What do you get when you cross a chick with a
Slinky?**

A: A spring chicken.

Warning! Don't spell *Part A* backwards. It's a trap.

Most people don't keep their New Year's resolutions.
They go in one year and out the other.

Q: What do you call a newborn female plant?

A: A Girl Sprout.

Knock, knock.
Who's there?
Spell.
Spell who?
Okay, W-H-O.

Q: What did the hot fudge say to the ice cream?

A: "Don't worry, I've got you covered."

Bo: They're not going to make yardsticks any longer.

Iris: Really?

Bo: Yeah, they're going to keep them at three feet.

My recliner and I go way back.

Don: What do you call a string bean that got old?
Jon: A has-bean.

Q: What do you call a girl who's in the middle of a tennis court?

A: Annette.

Q: What state has the smallest soft drinks?

A: Mini-soda.

I've started telling everyone about the benefits of eating dried grapes. It's all about raisin awareness.

Rick: How do you get a farmer's daughter to fall for you?

Nick: A tractor.

Mary: Why can't you ever call the zoo?
Shari: 'Cause the lion is always busy.

I lost my voice. I'm sorry, I can't talk about it.

A little boy was going to bed during a loud thunderstorm. He sat up and asked his mom, "Will you sleep with me tonight?"

"I can't," she answered. "I have to sleep with Daddy."

"So, he's scared too?" the boy said. "The big baby."

Bo: I'm sorry I gave you a bad haircut.

Joe: That's okay; I'll keep it under my hat.

Ed: Why did the horse talk with his mouth full?

Ted: Because he had bad stable manners.

Mike: Why did the music students get in trouble?
Ike: They were caught passing notes!

Crushing soft drink cans can be soda pressing.

Jason: What kind of fish fixes your grand piano?
Mason: A piano tuna.

Bill: I accidently plugged my electric blanket into the toaster last night.

Will: What happened?

Bill: I spent all night popping out of bed.

Tim: Why was the ice cream lonely?

Jim: Because the banana split.

Q: What bet can never be won?

A: The alphabet.

Q: What did the hot dog say to the tomato?

A: "Let's get together soon so we can ketchup."

Q: What does a farmer say when he starts a party?

A: "Lettuce turnip the beet!"

Knock, knock.
Who's there?

Baron.
Baron who?

Baron mind who you're talking to.

Knock, knock.
Who's there?

Avery.
Avery who?

Avery time I come over to your house we go through this!

Knock, knock.
Who's there?

Ben.
Ben who?

Ben knocking on this door all morning!

Knock, knock.
Who's there?

Canoe.
Canoe who?

Canoe come out and play?

This cheese saved the entire world! It was legend dairy.

Ben: What do you call a clumsy letter?
Len: A bumble *B*.

Macy: Why did the vegetable boat sink?
Lacey: It was full of leeks!

Who brought all these leeks?!?

Teacher: Name five things that contain milk.
    Kid: Butter, cheese, ice cream, and . . . two cows!

Mary: Why did you stop dating the seismologist?
Shari: He was too quick to find faults.

Is a kid who's refusing to nap resisting a rest?

Got a job as a historian but realized there was no future in it.

Two guys went to the movies together. One brought his dog. The friend was amazed because the dog seemed to follow the story, laughing in all the right places and getting really quiet at the sad parts. After the movie, the friend couldn't stand it anymore. He said, "This is amazing. Your dog seemed to actually enjoy the movie!"

"Yeah, I was shocked," the dog owner said. "He hated the book."

Q: Why didn't the baseball player score any points?

A: He kept running home.

Ben: Why did the opera singer need a ladder?
Jen: She wanted to reach the high notes.

I used to wear winter gloves all the time. Now I only wear them intermittenly.

Pat: What do you call a can opener that won't work?

Matt: A can't opener.

Exaggerations went up by a million percent last month.

My friend invented an invisible airplane, but I can't see it taking off.

Bill: What do you call 30 pandas playing musical chairs?

Jill: Panda-monium.

Customer: This bread you sold me is full of holes!

Baker: What do you expect? It's hole wheat bread.

Q: What do you call a Frenchman wearing sandals?

A: Phillipe Phillop.

When you were growing up, how small was your house?

It was so small I had to go outside to change my mind.

It was so small the mice were hunchbacked.

When I stuck the key in the front door, I broke the back window.

When I turned around, I was next door.

I ordered a large pizza and had to eat it outside.

When I stepped through the front door, I was in the backyard.

When I dropped a tissue, I got wall-to-wall carpeting.

When we ate in the kitchen, our elbows were in the living room.

Tongue Twisters

She sees cheese.

Dust is a disc's worst enemy.

Can you scan a can the way a can scanner can?

Betty and Bob brought back blue balloons from the big bazaar.

Rubber baby buggy bumpers.

Knock, knock.
Who's there?

Snow.
Snow who?

Snow fun to do my homework.

I love jokes about eyes. The cornea the better.

A guy tried to sell me a mirror, but I knew it was a scam. I could see right through it.

To the guy who stole my glasses: I will find you. I have contacts.

Knock, knock.
Who's there?

Kayak.
Kayak who?

Kayak with you about something?

I was driving my bread car when it caught on fire. Now it's toast.

I swapped our bed for a trampoline. My wife hit the roof.

Q: How do meteorologists go up a mountain?
A: They climate.

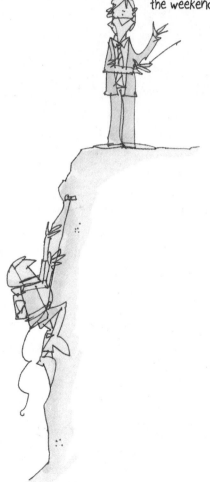

Two guys fell down a hole. One said, "Wow, it's dark in here, isn't it?"

The other one answered, "I don't know; I can't see."

Kid: Dad, can you tell me what a solar eclipse is?
Dad: No sun.

Q: Which one of Santa's reindeer has bad manners?

A: Rude-olph.

I got a compliment on my driving. Someone left a note on my windshield that said, "Parking fine."

Q: Why did the kid drop veggies all over his map of the world?

A: He wanted peas on earth.

Q: What yummy snack is always speaking?

A: A talk-o.

Q: What does the cat like on her toast in the morning?

A: Orange meow-malade.

Q: What's a cat's favorite brand of diapers?

A: Pam-purrs.

Two boys went with their parents to a wedding. As they watched the proceedings, one turned to the other and whispered, "How many wives can a man have?"

"I don't know, why?"

"So far I've counted sixteen."

"Sixteen?"

"Yeah—four better, four worse, four richer, four poorer."

Flo: Thanks for hooking up my dog and taking him for a walk.

Joe: No problem. It's the leash I could do.

Q: What superhero likes freshly pressed clothes?
A: Iron Man.

Q: What's a kitten's favorite subject in school?
A: Mewsic.

Knock, knock.
Who's there?
Cattle.
Cattle who?
Cattle purr if you pet her.

Terry: How did Mickey Mouse save Minnie from drowning?
Jerry: He gave her mouse-to-mouse resuscitation.

Asher: What do you get when you cross a cocker spaniel, a poodle, and a rooster?

Harper: A cocker-poodle-do.

Andy: Where did the Wright Brothers' cat invent the airplane?

Randy: Kitty Hawk.

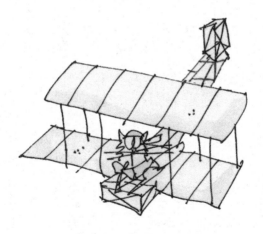

Q: What do a boat captain and a hatmaker have in common?

A: They're both concerned with capsizing.

Q: Where do young chickens go on vacation?

A: Chickago.

Jonny: Mom, can I go out and play?

Mom: What? With those holes in your sock?

Jonny: No, with the kids next door.

Q: What's a cheerleader's favorite cereal?

A: Cheerios!

Q: What's a turkey's favorite holiday?

A: Feather's Day.

Q: Why did the builder hire chickens to work on his crew?

A: They were cheep labor.

Q: What do you call a company that makes just average stuff?

A: A satis-factory.

Q: What does the Easter Bunny grow in his garden?

A: Eggplants.

Q: Why does the chef always laugh while he's making breakfast?

A: Because the egg always cracks a yolk.

Q: Why was the calendar so jumpy?

A: It was a leap year.

Q: Where do penguins go to see movies?

A: The dive-in.

Q: Why was the grizzly turned away from the restaurant?

A: Because there were no bear feet allowed.

Q: Why did the socks move to the fruit orchard?

A: They liked living in pears.

Q: What does a buffalo wear to the pool?

A: Bison-glasses.

Q: Where do cats wait to pay their bills?

A: In the fee line.

Teacher: How long does it take to make butter?
Farm Boy: An echurnity!

I told my doctor I broke my arm in two places. He told me to avoid those places.

Teacher: What kind of nut has no shell?
Benjamin: A doughnut!

I understand how cars work, but airplanes are way over my head.

The best time on a clock is 6:30, hands down.

Kid: Mom, there's going to be a small PTA meeting tonight.

Mom: What do you mean "small"?

Kid: Just you, me, and the principal.

Q: What kind of cheese likes to shoot hoops?

A: *Swish* cheese.

You can take a horse to water, but a pencil must be led.

Len: Why should you always bring chips to a party?

Ben: In queso emergency.

Q: How do monkeys stay in shape?

A: They go to the jungle gym.

Chloe: What's a frog's favorite restaurant?
Kylie: IHOP.

Just went to an outdoor wedding and it rained the entire time. The whole thing was in tents.

Q: What kind of tree can fit in your hand?

A: A palm tree.

Ben: A king had three goblets. Two were full and one was half full. What was the king's name?

Len: I give up.

Ben: Phillip the Third!

Q: What is a computer tech's favorite dessert?

A: Apple pie à la modem.

Q: What do you call a knight who's afraid to fight?

A: Sir Render.

Man: I'd like to place a call to Wenatchee, Washington.

Operator: Can you spell that?

Man: If I could spell it, I'd write a letter.

People want the front of the bus, the back of the church, and the center of attention.

Knock, knock.
Who's there?
Iris.
Iris who?
Iris-eived a package in the mail. Was it from you?

Knock, knock.
Who's there?
Rita.
Rita who?
Rita good book lately?

Knock, knock.
Who's there?

Ira.
Ira who?

Ira-member you; do you remember me?

Tongue Twisters

Silly Sally swiftly shooed seven silly sheep.

Six sick hicks nick six slick bricks with picks and sticks.

Round the rough and rugged rock, the ragged rascal rudely ran.

Ed had edited it.

She sells seashells at the seashore. So, if she sells shells at the seashore, I'm sure she sells seashore shells.

Knock, knock.
Who's there?

Edith.
Edith who?

Edith thick juithy burger for me, will ya?

Knock, knock.
Who's there?

Alex.
Alex who?

Alex some more root beer, please.

Knock, knock.
Who's there?

Isabel.
Isabel who?

Isabel working or should I just keep knocking?

A city guy was renting a horse for the day. The wrangler asked, "Do you want a saddle horn?"

"Naw," the city guy answered. "I figure I won't run into much traffic."

Customer: What's that fly doing in my alphabet soup?

Waiter: Trying to learn to read?

Christy: I keep thinking today is Monday.

Misty: Today *is* Monday.

Christy: I know, that's why I keep thinking it.

Mom: Why do you keep burping?

Max: I had belchin' waffles for breakfast.

Teacher: Harper, please use the word *column* in a sentence.

Harper: When I want to talk to my friend, I column up on the phone.

Patient: Doc, to be honest, I don't feel any better since our last visit.

Doctor: Did you follow the directions on the bottle of medicine I gave you?

Patient: Sure did. The bottle said, "Keep tightly closed."

BACKWARD JOKES

Backward jokes give the answer first, then the question. Here's an example:

The answer is, *A paradox*.

The question is, *What do you call two surgeons walking down the hall?*

Answer: Rampage.

Question: What do they call a sheet in the LA football team's playbook?

Answer: Lumberjack.

Question: What do you call it when someone steals your lumber?

Answer: Semiconductor.

Question: What do you call a part-time orchestra leader?

Answer: Europe.

Question: What does the umpire say when it's your turn to bat?

Answer: Protein.

Question: What do you call a teenager who plays a sport for money?

Answer: Padlock.

Question: How does a frog keep his home secure?

Answer: Plymouth Rock.

Question: What kind of music did the pilgrims listen to?

Answer: Chicken coop.

Question: What does a chicken drive if the chicken sedan isn't available?

Answer: Ocean liner.

Question: What's another name for sand?

Answer: Polygon.

Question: What do you say when your parrot flies away?

Answer: A pup tent.

Question: What does Lassie take with her on campouts?

Answer: Submission.

Question: What do you call it when a submarine goes on a trip?

Answer: Babysitter.

Question: What's another name for a high chair?

Liam: Mom, you know that vase that's been handed down from generation to generation?

Mom: Yes.

Liam: Well, this generation dropped it.

Cop: You look like you were pushing 60.

Phyllis: How rude! I'm only 45.

Chef: I've been cooking for 25 years.
Diner: Then I guess my order is almost ready.

Kyle: Dad, I can't get the car started. I think it's flooded.
Dad: Where is it?
Kyle: In the swimming pool.

I sold my vacuum cleaner the other day. All it was doing was collecting dust.

Man: Doctor, you've got to help me! I'm convinced I'm a poodle.
Psychiatrist: How long have you felt like this?
Man: Ever since I was a puppy.

Dad: Well, son, you've got one thing in your favor.

Jon: What's that?

Dad: With this report card, you couldn't possibly be cheating.

Two businessmen sit down in a roadside diner.

Mac: I'd like a cup of coffee.

Jack: Me too, and make sure it's in a clean cup.

The waitress comes back a couple minutes later with their coffee.

Waitress: Okay, which one of you ordered a clean cup?

Q: What's a cop's favorite board game?

A: Monopolice.

Asher: What's a karate champion's favorite dish?
Harper: Kung food.

Q: What kind of key opens a banana?

A: A mon-key.

Q: What Olympic race is never run?

A: The swimming race.

Max: Why did you get that Good Drivers Award?
Caden: Because I was wreck-less.

I have a phobia of German sausage. I fear the wurst.

Bo: What did the dog say after a long day at work?
Iris: "Wow, today was ruff."

Ron: My dad's never done a day's work in his life.

Jon: Why not?

Ron: He's a night watchman.

Randy: What does a chicken need to finish a marathon?

Andy: Hen-durance.

Will: Why couldn't the chicken find her eggs?

Jill: 'Cause she mislaid them.

Ed: What do chickens serve at birthday parties?

Ned: Coop-cakes.

Jason: What time do chickens go to bed?

Mason: At half past hen.

Did you hear that the invisible man married the invisible woman? Their kids aren't much to look at either.

Q: What flower rules the garden?

A: The dande-lion.

Q: What do baby kangaroos wear?

A: Jumpsuits.

Q: What do snakes take for a cold?

A: Anti-hiss-tamines.

My fear of moving stairs is escalating.

Q: Why did the laptop get glasses?

A: To improve his web-sight.

Remy: I fell off my horse in the barn this afternoon.

Charlotte: Are you okay?

Remy: Yeah, the doctor said my condition was stable.

Deagan: Left my glasses at home yesterday. Guess who I bumped into?

Hannah: Who?

Deagan: Everyone!

Mom: Brandon, what was that?
Brandon: My shirt fell on the ground.
Mom: Why was it so loud?
Brandon: I was in it.

Q: How do ducks celebrate the Fourth of July?
A: With firequackers.

Q: Who's the pig's favorite movie star?
A: Kevin Bacon.

Q: What do you call a helicopter with a skunk inside?
A: A smelly-copter.

Q: Where do cows, chickens, and horses get their medications?

A: At Old MacDonald's Farmacy.

**Q: What do you get when you cross a pig with a
newscaster?**

A: An oinkerman.

And now here's the news...

Son: Dad, I want to drive a tank in the army.
Dad: Well, I won't stand in your way.

Principal: Why were you acting up in orchestra class?

Connor: I just didn't know how to conduct myself.

Q: What has 100 legs and says, "Ho, ho, ho"?

A: A Santa-pede.

Knock, knock.
Who's there?

Comma.
Comma who?

Comma little closer and see for yourself.

Knock, knock.
Who's there?

Harmony.
Harmony who?

Harmony times do I need to knock on the door before you let me in?

Q: What do you get when you cross a bunny with a flatbread sandwich?

A: Pita Rabbit.

I lost another audiobook. Now I'll never hear the end of it.

Terry: Why did you get fired from the computer keyboard factory?

Jerry: I wasn't putting in enough shifts.

Did you hear my new song about tortillas? Actually, it's more of a wrap.

Chloe: What rock group has four guys who don't sing?

Kylie: Mount Rushmore.

A snail was riding on a turtle's back when it crashed into another turtle. The cop asked the snail what happened. He said, "I don't know; it all happened so fast!"

I ordered a chicken and an egg off the internet just to see which came first.

Why did you lose your job?

Barber: Kept taking shortcuts.
Doctor: Was short on patients.
Taxi Driver: Kept driving my customers away.

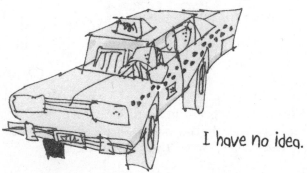

Moving-Van Driver: Got carried away with my work.
Dentist: I was always looking down in the mouth.
Coin-Mint Worker: I stopped making cents.
Giraffe Feeder at the Zoo: I wasn't up to the task.
Worker in an Origami Store: I worked there until it folded.

Q: What do you call a snail who joins the Navy?

A: A snailor.

We're collecting vegetable jokes. If you have any, lettuce know.

Q: Where do pig Eskimos live?

A: In pigloos!

Q: What kind of tree does a math teacher climb?

A: A geometry!

I went on a once-in-a-lifetime vacation. Never again.

Bo: Which is faster: hot or cold?
Iris: Hot, because you can always catch a cold.

Time is what keeps things from happening all at once.

Q: Why did the pony get sent to the principal's office?

A: He was horsing around.

Isabel: Why did the bee get married?
Rose: Because he found his honey!

When tempted to fight fire with fire, remember that the fire department usually uses water.

Teacher: Steven, how far were you from the right
answer?

Steven: Just two seats.

Q: What's brown, hairy, and wears sunglasses?

A: A coconut on vacation.

**Q: Why doesn't the farmer's dog like his sheep
jokes?**

A: Because he's herd them all.

Q: What is a tornado's favorite game to play?

A: Twister!

Q: What's green and wears a cape?

A: Super Pickle.

Q: What did the big flower say to the little flower?

A: "Hi, bud."

Braedon: What does bread do on the weekends?

Caden: Just loafs around.

Asher: What does a flower say when it's teasing?
Harper: "I'm just pollen your leg."

Max: What do you call a flamingo at the North Pole?
Alsea: Lost.

I was wondering
if you can help me . . .

Ava: How do you fix a broken tomato?
Rowan: With tomato paste.

Knock, knock.
Who's there?
Chicken.
Chicken who?
Chicken your pockets; your keys might be in there.

Man: Doctor, I'm convinced I'm an elevator!
Psychiatrist: Can you come in to see me immediately?
Man: I can't; I don't stop at your floor!

Two artists had an art contest. It ended in a draw.

Donny: Where do fish sleep?
Ronny: In a riverbed.

I tried to sue the airline for losing my luggage. I lost my case.

Tad: Why did the boy bring a ladder to the football game?

Rad: He heard the Giants were playing.

Do you think Earth makes fun of other planets for having no life?

Boss: Can you come in on Saturday? I really need you.

Steven: Sure, but I might be a little late. Buses are slow on the weekend.

Boss: What time will you get here?

Steven: Monday.

Sal: Why did the two fours skip dinner?
Hal: They already eight!

Jack: Why did the vegetable gardener quit her job?
Zach: Her celery wasn't high enough.

Brian: A year ago, my doctor told me I was losing my hearing.

Ryan: What happened?

Brian: I haven't heard from him since.

Lyle: What happened to you?

Kyle: I broke my leg raking leaves.

Lyle: How did you do that?

Kyle: Fell out of the tree.

Q: What did the dalmatian say after he ate his dinner?

A: "That hit the spot."

Hannah: Why are you putting that cake in the freezer?

Deagan: The recipe says to ice it after baking.

Mason: Why shouldn't you talk to a broken pencil?

Jason: It's pointless.

Bob: How do you make more room for pigs on a farm?

Rob: Build a sty-scraper.

Charlotte: Where do polar bears vote?
  Remy: The North Poll.

Patient: Doctor, I'm convinced I'm an alligator!
Doctor: Well, can you come in next week? Right now, I'm swamped.

Knock, knock.
Who's there?

An author.
An author who?

An author joke like this and I'm outta here!

Emily Biddle's Little-Known Book Titles

Digging into Ancient History **by R. K. Ology**

It's Your Choice! **by Howard U. Lykett**

I'm Tired of Schoolwork! **by Anita Vacation**

Communicating with Cows **by I. Ken Moo**

Would You Like a Million Dollars? **by Sherwood B. Nice**

Learn How to Dance **by Tristin Shout**

I'm Just Kidding! **by Shirley U. Jest**

Discovering Dinosaurs **by Tara Dacktill**

Raising Pigs, Goats, and Cattle **by Iona Farm**

Getting Close to Bees **by I. Ben Stung**

More Books in Emily's Collection

The World's Easiest Diet **by M. T. Cupboards**

How I Crossed the Sahara **by Rhoda Camel**

Working at the Gas Station **by Phil R. Upp**

Ham on Rye **by Della Catessen**

Who Saw Him Go? **by Wendy Leave**

101 Recipes **by R. U. Hungry**

Simple Household Fixes **by Andy Mann**

The Laser Battle **by Ray Gunn**

Awake All Night **by Constance Noring**

Exploring the South Pole **by Anne Arctic**

Sandy Silverthorne, author of *Crack Yourself Up Jokes for Kids*, *More Crack Yourself Up Jokes for Kids*, and *Made You Laugh!*, has been writing and illustrating books since 1988 and currently has over 800,000 copies in print. His award-winning Great Bible Adventure children's series with Harvest House sold over 170,000 copies and has been distributed in eight languages worldwide. His One-Minute Mysteries series has sold over 240,000 copies. He's written and illustrated over 30 books and has worked with such diverse clients as Universal Studios Tour, Doubleday Publishers, Penguin, World Vision, the University of Oregon, the Charlotte Hornets, and the Academy of Television Arts and Sciences. Sandy has worked as a cartoonist, author, illustrator, actor, pastor, speaker, and comedian. Apparently, it's hard for him to focus. Connect with him at sandysilverthornebooks.com.

Learn More about
SANDY

Head to **sandysilverthornebooks.com**
for jokes, Bible stories and lessons,
drawing tutorials, and more!

And follow Sandy on social media:

 sandsilver

 SandySilverthornesPage

 Sandy Silverthorne

READY FOR MORE LAUGHS?

Revell
a division of Baker Publishing Group
www.RevellBooks.com